SILENT VOICES

recent American
poems on nature

Library of Congress Cataloging in Publication Data
Main entry under title:

Silent voices.

   1. American poetry—20th century.
          2. Nature—Poetry. I. Feroe, Paul.
PS615.S468   811'.5'408   78-54317
ISBN 0-915408-18-X
ISBN 0-915408-17-1 pbk.

Copyright © 1978 by the Ally Press
Published by the Ally Press,
P.O. Box 30340, St. Paul, MN 55175
Manufactured in the United States of America.
Cover design by Hal Aqua.

Other titles from The Ally Press:
I Never Wanted Fame, Antonio Machado, translated by
Robert Bly
The Voices, Rainer Maria Rilke, translated by Robert Bly
The Red, White and Blue Poem, Susan Fromberg Schaeffer
Try To Live To See This!, Kabir, versions by Robert Bly
The Playfair Book of Hours, Norbert Krapf (o.p.)
Yogh, Martin Booth

ACKNOWLEDGMENTS

Susan Astor: "The Farmer Lost A Child" first appeared in the *Chowder Review*, 1976.

Robert Bly: "Night Farmyard" is reprinted from *Old Man Rubbing His Eyes* and appears by permission of Unicorn Press, copyright © Robert Bly, 1976. "The Dead Seal near McClure's Beach" and "Looking at a Dry Tumbleweed Brought in from the Snow" are from *The Morning Glory* by Robert Bly. Copyright © 1975 by Robert Bly. By permission of Harper & Row, Publishers, Inc.

Joe Bruchac: "November Rain," "The Rivers," "Rain in July" and "In the Garden," first appeared in a chapbook *This Earth Is A Drum*, 1976, and appear courtesy of the publisher, Cold Mountain Press.

Philip Dacey: "The Cat," "The Rise and Fall," "The Steps Animals Take," and "The Animal's Christmas," are reprinted from *How I Escaped From the Labyrinth and Other Poems*, copyright © 1977 by Philip Dacey, and appear by permission of Carnegie-Mellon University Press.

W.D. Ehrhart: "The Death of Kings" first appeared in *Rootless*, published by Samisdat Press, copyright © 1977.

Charles Fishman: "Warm-Blooded Animals" by permission of Northeast/Juniper Books; "Under Harsh Light" by permission of *Spree*, and "A Mourning Dove" by permission of *South & West*.

Frank Graziano: "Listening To The Sounds Of Spring Under Bamboo" first appeared in the *Red Cedar Review*.

Marjorie Hawksworth: "Knowing How Easily" first appeared in the Winter, 1977 edition of the *Carleton Miscellany*.

William Heyen: "The Spider" and "The Fourth Day" are reprinted from *Depth of Field*, copyright © 1970 by Baton Rouge: Lousiana State University Press. "The Snake," (first title "The Language") appeared first in *Service-berry*, copyright © William Heyen, 1978.

William Kloefkorn: "9." is reprinted from *Alvin Turner As Farmer*. "Uncertain The Final Run To Winter" is reprinted from *Uncertain The Final Run To Winter*. Both copyright © 1974 by Windflower Press.

Ted Kooser: "Fort Robinson," "Walking Beside A Creek," and "Sleeping Cat," reprinted from *Not Coming To Be Barked At*, copyright © 1976 by Ted Kooser. By permission of Pentagram Press. "Spring Plowing" reprinted from *A local habitation & a name*, copyright © 1974 by Ted Kooser. By permission of Solo Press.

Denise Levertov: "Come Into Animal Presence" reprinted from *The Jacob's Ladder*, copyright © 1961 by Denise Levertov Goodman. By permission of New Directions.

Duane Locke: "A Night In Late December," "An Evening Spent On A Georgia Farm," and "By a Gator Canal During The Dry Season," copyright © 1975 by Duane Locke. Reprinted from *Poems From The Starfish Mss.*, Ann Arbor Review Press.

Steven Osterlund: "Tiger" and "Running Horse" first appeared in *Poetry Now*. "Butterfly" first appeared in *The New Salt Creek Reader*. By permission of the author. All are forthcoming in a book from Open Chord Press.

Anthony Piccione: "Late Autumn," "Poem Touching The Feet," "Camping Alone" and "Rising Early In Winter" are reprinted from *Anchor Dragging*, forward by Archibald McLeach, copyright © 1977 by Anthony Piccione. By permission of Boa Editions.

Kenneth Rexroth: "Another Spring" and "Human, Avian, Vegetable Blood" are reprinted from *Collected Shorter Poems*, copyright © 1966 by New Directions Publishing Corporation. By permission of New Directions.

Joanne Seltzer: "Poem Watching in Winter" first appeared in a 1977 issue of the *Berkshire Arts and Leisure Magazine*.

Gary Snyder: "The Dead By The Side of The Road," reprinted from *Turtle Island*, copyright © 1974 by Gary Snyder. "Long Hair" reprinted from *Regarding Wave*, copyright © 1970 by Gary Snyder. Both reprinted by permission of New Directions.

David Spicer: "Swans" first appeared in *Moondance*.

Lucien Stryk: "Farmer" and "Cormorant" are reprinted from *Selected Poems*, copyright © 1967 by Lucien Stryk. By permission of Swallow Press.

Michael Waters: "Remembering The Oak" (Four Quarters) and "Black Leaves" (The Missouri Review) both appeared in *The Scent of Apples*, copyright © 1977 by Croissant Company. "If I Die" has appeared in *Poetry* and also in *In Memory of Smoke*, Rook Press, 1977.

Nancy Willard: "Iris," "When There Were Trees," and "Moss" first appeared in *Carpenter of the Sun* (Liveright) and are reprinted by permission of the author.

James Wright: "A Blessing," "Milkweed," and "Fear Is What Quickens Me," copyright © 1961, 1962 by James Wright. Reprinted from *The Branch Will Not Break* by permission of Wesleyan University Press. "A Blessing" first appeared in *Poetry*.

Grateful thanks to Julie Nelson and
Norbert Krapf for their help and
encouragement with this production.

SILENT VOICES

Recent American poems on nature

Edited by Paul Feroe

Ally Press * St. Paul * Minnesota

TABLE OF CONTENTS

INTRODUCTION

In this country's ancestral days human survival was grounded in nature and communion with it was sacred and intense. The animals in the forest and even the forest itself played a vital role in man's society. Indian cultures regarded all living things as part of an integrated whole, bestowing divinity on places and creatures. Some, like the Sioux, identified so closely with animals that they did not give them a generic term, instead calling them "the brothers that swim" and "the brothers that fly."

Only 300 years ago settlers arrived with a cultural system that designated European man as the supreme life-force, a status he felt allowed him to ride roughshod over the rights of the North American habitants. In only a few decades a fixation on economic and territorial trowth destroyed the careful balance of nature worked out by previous cultures, and with it the sense of the sacredness of life cherished by the Indians.

Psychiatrist Carl Jung observed that Western material growth developed at a cost to psychic well-being. He felt that our mutual past with nature gives modern man an inherent need to relate spiritually to it and that the spiritual dryness that has accompanied the rise of our culture is a result of an offensive attitude towards nature.

Man feels himself isolated in the cosmos, because he is no longer involved in nature and has lost his emotional "unconscious identity" with natural phenomena. These have slowly lost their symbolic implications...No river contains a spirit, no tree is the life principle of a man, no snake the embodiment of wisdom...No voices now speak to man from stones, plants and animals, nor does he speak to them believing they can hear. His contact with nature is gone, and with it has gone the profound emotional energy that this symbolic connection supplied.*

Fortunately, the break with nature Jung describes is not irreversable. In the last two decades poets have reflected in their work a renewed concern for the environment, expressed nationwide by various back-to-nature movements. As antenna of the culture these writers share the themes of the movement and illuminate a path to psychic wholeness that includes a reverence for all life.

This collection is meant to capture the spirit and sensitivity of a new awareness and to demonstrate the underlying importance of wildlife and animals to our lives. These poems do not simply give us an appreciation of nature, they relate the interaction of man with his environment and challenge us to recognize the depth and completeness of non-human existence. Moreover, they ask that we re-approach our own lives with a similar sense of awe.

Whereas modern poetry has sometimes seemed inaccessible, these poems speak to everyone and their clarity and intensity have the potential to carry the reader beyond himself and into contact with the oneness of nature. Reading them, we awaken to nature's *silent voices,* their message and their hope.

Paul Feroe

* Carl G. Jung. *Man and His Symbols.* New York: Dell Publishing Co. Inc., 1964. Page 65.

"Is not the sky a father and the earth a mother, and are not all living things with feet or wings or roots their children?"

Black Elk

from *Black Elk Speaks*

SEA PEOPLE

Above and under, over and below,
The limbless mammals
Stroke the sea.

Day bubbles upward through the dark,
Night settles down
And still they move;
Warmed by their own warm blood,
They meet and rub
In the ocean's vast room.

Who are these porpoises and whales,
Who, unencumbered, pulse and wallop
Over shells and tentacles,
Past skitters of slim fish,
Around the islands of our continents
Loving without lips,
Nursing without noise...?

We pile our cities up like blocks
And climb them, chattering,
While underneath
The vowel-voiced animals
Just swim
And arch their bodies into smiles.

Susan Astor

THE FARMER LOST A CHILD

She milks the cow at midnight,
Resting her head against the warm brown flank.
Everywhere, creatures
tongue and rustle in the dark barn.
The nudge of their disquiet makes her steady
As she stirs a pail of gruel to soothe the pigs,
Pebbles the skittish chickens with a fine feed.
Then, numb and purposeful,
She plows the fields for hours,
Combing the damp, tendrilled acreage,
Braiding the harvest.
The low moon lays her shadow
In a long path back to the house.

Day breaks on schedule;
The wheels of waking turn evenly.
Only she, off kilter with a bubble of pain,
Breaks rhythm,
Halts to a lopsided sleep.

Susan Astor

NIGHT FARMYARD

The horse lay on his knees sleeping.
A rat hopped across the scattered hay
and disappeared under the henhouse.
There the chickens sat in a stiff darkness.

Asleep they are like bark fallen from an old cottonwood.
Yet we know their soul is gone, risen
far into the upper air about the moon.

Robert Bly

THE DEAD SEAL NEAR McCLURE'S BEACH

1.

Walking north toward the point, I came on a dead seal. From a few feet away he looks like a brown log. The body is on its back, dead only a few hours. I stand and look at him. There's a quiver in the dead flesh. My God he is still alive. A shock goes through me, as if a wall of my room had fallen away.

His head is arched, the small eyes closed, the whiskers sometimes rise and fall. He is dying. This is the oil. Here on its back is the oil that heats our houses so efficiently. Wind blows fine sand back toward the ocean. The flipper near me lies folded over the stomach, looking like an unfinished arm, lightly glazed with sand at the edges. The other flipper lies half underneath. The seal's skin looks like an old overcoat, scratched here and there, by sharp mussel-shells maybe . . .

I reach out and touch him. Suddenly he rears up, turns over, gives three cries, Awaark! Awaark! Awaark! —like the cries from Christmas toys. He lunges toward me. I am terrified and leap back, although I know there can be no teeth in that jaw. He starts flopping toward the sea. But he falls over, on his face. He does not want to go back to the sea. He looks up at the sky, and he looks like an old lady who has lost her hair.

He puts his chin back on the sand, rearranges his flippers, and waits for me to go. I go.

2.

Today I go back to say goodbye; he's dead now. But he's not—he's a quarter mile farther up the shore. Today he is thinner, squatting on his stomach, head out. The ribs show more—each vertebra on the back under the coat is now visible, shiny. He breathes in and out.

He raises himself up, and tucks his flippers under, as if to keep them warm. A wave comes in, touches his nose. He turns and looks at me—the eyes slanted, the crown of his head is like a black leather jacket. He is taking a long time to die. The whiskers white as porcupine quills, the forehead slopes...goodbye brother, die in the sound of waves, forgive us if we have killed you, long live your race, your inner-tube race, so uncomfortable on land, so comfortable in the ocean. Be comfortable in death then, where the sand will be out of your nostrils, and you can swim in long loops through the pure death, ducking under as assassinations break above you. You don't want to be touched by me. I climb the cliff and go home the other way.

Robert Bly

A MAN AND A WOMAN AND A BLACKBIRD

"A man and a woman are one. A man and a woman and
a blackbird are one." So when we feel the union, then the
law of three leaps in, so many nights in our twenties, alone
on interior mountains, forgotten. A man and a woman are
sitting in a room. Outdoors the blackbirds whistle in the
deep snow, for "the blackbirds are involved with what I
know."

Out in the snow is what we do not know, the constella-
tions we have not seen yet, that the pig sees past his wild
snout, those areas beyond understanding that the heron
feels with his wing tip feathers stretched out in the air
above the flooded lake.

A man and a woman are sitting in a room. On the win-
dow pane, ice. The man says: "How is it I have never
loved ice before?" This faint cloudy blanket of ice that the
window hugs to itself - a cloak that the pane called out of
the air - this blanket is the closeness of all things to us, even
the coldest, the far-off pharoahs, and the bucket-headed
beasts that the vulture celebrates over... All of these lie
out beyond the ice. But when the union comes, and the
rivers join in the cloudy chamber, then they too join us,
and we too hang our harps on the willows, and the willow
joins us, and the man and the woman and the blackbird are
one.

—Robert Bly

Looking at a Dry Tumbleweed Brought in from the Snow

What is this wonderful thing? Brown and everywhere! It has leaped up on my desk like surf, or like a bull onto a cow! It rushes everywhere in front of me. . . . And my sleeping senses are shouted at, called in from the back of my head, to look at it! Well, it is only a broken-off bush, a tumbleweed, every branch different, and the whole bush the same, so in that way it is like the sea. Taken in from the deserted shore, it talks of queens sent away to live in cramped farmhouses, living in the dirt, and it talks of coffins and amazing arrows, no it is a love, some love we forget every day, it is my mother.

Robert Bly

IN THE GARDEN

The racks where tomatoes grew
still stand, ash poles
glazed with ice.
Spring will come again before
I take up that spading fork,
held in frozen Earth,
forgotten on a lazy fall afternoon.
Its wood is turning
grey as old bone.

As I walk, my feet
break through the crust,
the way seeds drop
into the furrows of early June,
falling the way
the old people fell
into the soil
with a thousand
generations of Corn.

Joe Bruchac

RAIN IN JULY

Clouds, someone said,
are the thoughts of Heaven.

This Sunday morning,
the sky thought of rain.

When I look down
from my study window
I see the soil
dark as swamp mud
from the rain that fell
all through the night
and still falls,
light, slow, soaking.

The carrot tops are green mist,
the corn leaves hold drops
of shining quartz.
Roots move towards
the darkness of ripening
and everything green
has become greener.

When I cross the lawn
barefooted,
I laugh at myself,
running so that my feet
will not take root
with the grass.

Joe Bruchac

THE RIVERS

Countless strands of thread gather
shimmering under the falling day star,
a magic.

Drop stone among stone
and pieces still can be named,
but rain or tears,
the flow of a stream,
a glass of water
fall into the river
and become themselves no longer.

Nothing else has such magic as this—
except that river
made of the breath
of animals, plants
and the moist Earth.

In it every place
is downstream,
all around you
is the sea.

Joe Bruchac

12.

NOVEMBER RAIN

Falls toward the door
of another season,
that long-held breath
which begins with first frost
and will not be released
until the green sigh of leaves.

One drop strikes my hand
and melts into the small hairs,
another strikes my face
and my eyes ache
for one clear moment
with a vision of voyaging
and a distant morning.

Joe Bruchac

THE STEPS ANIMALS TAKE

The steps animals take
are over our
bodies.
The great
spiritual

bellies
passing over
us. They are a constant
roof leaving us
exposed.

Like massive
guardian angels,
dressed in flowing
garments of blood,
they step carefully;

not once have they
crushed a life.
With no sky but their
gleaming undersides, no walls
but their bright shanks,

we walk in the midst
of a herd, its violence
translated
into a precise
dance.

Philip Dacey

THE RISE AND FALL

The rise and fall
at the chest
of an animal.
There is patience
buried near some bellows

begun with time.
A continuing, precisely
right rhythm.
Thought has never
known such slow

steps:
the dance inside
caves of bone,
inhuman
repetitions

of love.
Still they move
with such surpassing
violence,
and explain

nothing.
Translate them!
Translate
the raised hoof.
Read me their story.

Philip Dacey

THE ANIMAL'S CHRISTMAS

They are always living
in Christmas.
Though they walk years
through a field
they can never step

out of the birth of a god.
In each dark brain
a star
sending light through their sinews
leads their hooves

forward from one miracle
to another,
the gleams
tipping grass
like the bright eyes

of uncountable millions
of babies
a field has borne.
When they rub a tree,
a secret myrrh

descends onto their backs.
They carry it and offer it
without even trying.
From their nostrils
they breathe good news.

Philip Dacey

16.

THE CAT

He has a history
of long, silent
descending
from trees.
He lands

years later
in the laps of women.
He brings with him
a memory
of waiting deep in leaves,

of bright claws he now
is amazed to find
grown short and tucked
like pale fingers
into the folds of a dress.

He has fallen
out of a life.
He tries to remember
a lake in a clearing,
but each time he would drink

from that memory
he discovers
in a blue saucer of milk
his face like a head
served up on a plate.

Philip Dacey

THE DEATH OF KINGS

> *"...tell sad stories of the death of kings."*
> —Shakespeare

Giant;
sleek master of the oceans:
you alone command
the land beyond the land.
What else could Jonah have feared
more than the will of God?
Who else could have broken iron Ahab?
Even irreverent Hobbes
paid you the highest respect.

Light gets lost
trying to find you, beating
ever more faintly on your black door,
the black wall of your kingdom
where you alone command.

The harpooneers wait on the surface,
patient as lean cats.
They dare not seek you in your own world,
but they know they do not have to:
in the end they will win,
and we shall have one more kingdom
empty of kings.

W.D. Ehrhart

TREES STANDING SENTRY

Geese dreaming north drift
in the sheer ozone of starlight

no planes snarl across
that silence

not one blade of grass springs back
under a passing foot

trees standing sentry growl
from their roots

each bough lifts its claws
toward the thorn-flower moon

each crown stares back at the blind
kings of the axe with eyes

like wolves

Charles Fishman

UNDER HARSH LIGHT

But as for you, most odious—
Would Blake call you holy?
          —Roethke, "Slug"

On the white wall, under harsh light,
slugs arrange themselves like apostrophes
and questionmarks: they are slick and dark
and silent as miniature whales

They plunge through a time-surf, twined
like threads on a screw: coiled and cool
but appearing hot as twinned candles
melting down to wax, dripping and congealing

at once   From under their seeking mouths
beams of pale light enter the world we
breathe in: tails of comets or corposants?
egg tubes or lasers?   Everything is still

but them   They move through their dance
needing no masks or drums but, knowing all
the steps, continue to the end   To live
like them!

night-engendered, cool as rock   to light
the sky like a soothsayer's comet!   to crawl
towards the unimaginable...and make it back!

Charles Fishman

A MOURNING DOVE

The dove roosts on the highway,
cooing its dark thoughts, looking
more like a decoy than a live
bird. When the car burns
rubber, under some hot hand,
the dove wakes, ruffles its feathers,
begins to lift: it is not ready
for that shining speed, that weight.

After, the mate alights, dodging
traffic, frantic, entirely alert:
it nudges the unresponsive head
beside it, dodges, nudges, dodges,
and does not fly.

Nothing we've learned will make
the dove rise.

Charles Fishman

WARM-BLOODED ANIMALS

The elk's massive beauty, the speed
of the unbridled horse,
the bearing of the cougar—
and its claws—
the fox's loyalty, the weasel's potency,
the crow's raucous call.

The knowledge that they have not yielded,
their fierce indifference to our
survival,
the harsh musk of their untamed cells.

Charles Fishman

GATHERING HERBS ON
IMMORTAL'S MOUNTAIN

This is spring
Orion rising
from a magpies breast
the pine trees
pointing toward evening
when your basket
is full
the weight makes you buckle
a bed of needles
that the wind from the North
laid down
and as you sleep
a grave begins to open
around you
while the melissa weaves roots
to your heart.

Frank Graziano

These poems are written after Chinese masterpiece paintings from the Ming and Sung dynasties.

LISTENING TO THE SOUNDS OF
SPRING UNDER BAMBOO

From the rock
a wind rises to its feet
no one hears a word
the river that spoke
has laid down its music
the sun mixed its brown
in the air
but one bud
like an oyster
prys itself open
the sound
of cocoons unraveling.

Frank Graziano

24.

IN THE MORNING, BEFORE AN
EMBROIDERED DRESSER & MIRROR

Your husband is gazing
knee-deep in the river
the rapids looking
for a hole
in his coat
maybe the minnows
will swallow
his reflection
or the tide
crack his cheeks
in respect for the moon
or perhaps his image
will rise on the mist
and his heart leap out
to follow it.

Frank Graziano

BAMBOO

After the flutes
the fishing poles
the branch
walking as a cane
toward Ch'u
after the broadleaves
swell full of wind
like hummingbirds
and the ants
and the snakes taste
the tip of the root
after frost
after autumn undresses
the breasts of the foliage
bamboo with its bones
guards winter.

Frank Graziano

KNOWING HOW EASILY

The old rajah on his elephant
rides on a sea
of wrinkled skin.
The gray waves beneath
his little cask
swell with the constancy
of an aged woman's breast
as she lies beside her lover
of fifty years.
The brahmin
knowing how easily
one form slips into another
closes his eyes
and rocks to the elephant's amble.
He is aware
that in the soft dip and roll
of this large silver animal
water has disciplined itself
to walk on the land.

Marjorie Hawksworth

THE SPIDER

The spider hovers always
just above the land
and when it walks
your pulse quickens

and where it walks the world
grows silent, birds
abandon their nests, deer
rush headlong across the roads, mice

burrow deeper, even the wind
seems to die.
The spider is white, its legs
like rain lit in shafts

of sunlight. The spider spins webs
like the sun spins them
under the water. You have seen
its nets and vines of silk

swaying between clouds,
almost invisible, almost unreal.
You have mistaken its breath
for woodsmoke, its body

for a snowstorm on the horizon.
For once, enter the eye of the spider,
see what it sees, wait for
insects bigger than islands

to strum its web. Fear
what it fears. It is summer.
You are the hunted and the hunter.
but you are not alone.

Many have seen the white fur
in the joints of its legs.
Listen. The spider is poised
in the air above you.

William Heyen

THE SNAKE

In the center of Brockport,
above the banked rocks
along the Erie Canal,
on a wild grapevine's
largest leaf,
a young snake
coiled sleeping
in October sun.
I knelt near,
my skull's shadow
covering the leaf
and snake body blending
its symmetries of scales
green into the leaf.
When, as though I
were part of its sky,
it looked up,
lowered its head,
and slept again,
I closed my eyes,
hoping for the reptile's
attractive nothingness.
The snake's language,
of course, was wordless,
and I, as though this desire
were worth it,
as though the still
autumn water and vista
of yellow maples
demanded this oblivion,
began to drift

into the snake's sunburst brain,
until, for a few beats
of our hearts,
I joined it on its leaf.
But soon, as here
dimension of the human,
the world became its words again,
the Main Street mutter
of traffic *traffic,* even
mica on a rock, *mica.*
I looked, in time,
to see the leaf tremble,
the snake's mission
to be there
and then to disappear
beneath the rocks,
mine to coil it,
as I do here,
tighter again, and tighter,
against its grapeleaf.

William Heyen

THE FOURTH DAY

This day is different.
This is the fourth day.
For three days wind
has rattled the shocks of corn.
For three days the sun
has pressed upon a bird
whose corpse has been

brown as the blowing dirt.
But this is the fourth day.
Today, in air still as a vacuum,
the wren's body hums.
The maggots in the sockets of its eyes
are touched blue, like pale flames.
A tendril of blood

twines about its beak.
Today, unfolding a flower,
the sun kindles, spreads
the wren's feathers.
There are no names for such beauty
as the sun finds here.
The wren can rise no higher.

William Heyen

UNCERTAIN THE FINAL RUN TO WINTER

Summer,
a fat horse
tender against the spurs.

Now as the last edge of autumn
hangs precipiced in yellow on the trees
the animal sees the sudden space and shies.
I sense the ropy girth go loose:
uncertain the final run to winter.

Between the halt and the beginning
lies the gap,
familiar to the eye
as palm to pommel.

My lean horse balks: ahead,
the wide white skylessness of space.

Not knowing where mount and rider end,
or where they come together,
I see myself as statue weathered,
sitting its saddle like an Ichabod.

William Kloefkorn

9.

The baby's cough was still in my ears
When I shot the rabbit.
Maybe that was why I found it so easy
To pull the trigger. We needed
Every peavine our plot could muster.
I don't know, maybe I
Should never have started farming.
I just don't care to see blood
On the lettuce. But the baby's cough
Was deep and going deeper,
And more than onion soup seemed necessary,
So I shot the rabbit again and again,
Sliding a deheaded stove bolt
Down the barrel to dislodge
The smoke-smeared casing. Then
In winter the blood was bright
Upon the snow as I anticipated
Spring. But the rabbit
Was always there, like the rock,
Singular as buckshot. Still,
I did what I could to save the garden,
Even long after the baby was buried.
We needed its savings for other ailments,
Other medicines. So into the seasons
I fought the rabbits,
The chamber of my .12-gauge
Like a little throat, coughing.

William Kloefkorn

34.

SPRING PLOWING

West of Omaha, the freshly-plowed fields
steam in the night like lakes.
The smell of the earth floods over the roads.
The fieldmice are moving their nests
to the higher ground of fence-rows,
the old among them crying out to the owls
to take them all. The paths in the grass
are loud with the squeak of their carts.
They keep their lanterns covered.

Ted Kooser

WALKING BESIDE A CREEK

Walking beside a creek
in December, the black ice
windy with leaves,
you can feel the great joy
of the trees, their coats
thrown open like drunken men,
the lifeblood thudding
in their tight, wet boots.

Ted Kooser

FORT ROBINSON

When I visited Fort Robinson,
where Dull Knife and his Northern Cheyenne
were held captive that terrible winter,
the grounds crew was killing the magpies.

Two men were going from tree to tree
with sticks and ladders, poking the young birds
down from their nests and beating them to death
as they hopped about in the grass.

Under each tree where the men had worked
were twisted clots of matted feathers,
and above each tree a magpie circled,
crazily calling in all her voices.

We didn't get out of the car.
My little boy hid in the back and cried
as we drove away, into those ragged buttes
the Cheyenne climbed that winter, fleeing.

Ted Kooser

SLEEPING CAT

for Linda Ulrich

My cat is asleep on his haunches
like a sphinx. He has gone down cautiously
into an earlier life, holding a thread
of the old world's noises, and feeling his way
through the bones. The scratch of my pen
keeps the thread taut. When I finish
the poem, and the sound in the room goes slack,
the cat will come scampering back
into the blinding, bright rooms in his eyes.

Ted Kooser

CATALPA IN THE PARKING LOT

Stripped of its huge
heart-shaped leaves
which gave it
summer privacy

it stands straight
on the side of the street

the bark ridged
up and down as though
from insect trackways

the gnarled beanlike pods
packed with seeds
swaying heavily
against the sky

like the organs
of prehistoric animals.

Norbert Krapf

BITTERSWEET ALONG THE EXPRESSWAY

As if in retreat
from the unending lines
of cars jerking and
swerving from Manhattan
onto Long Island

the slender bushes
crawl up the wire fence
preserving the thin
strip of greenery
from the service road

and like wild animals
trapped in a zoo
peer through wire diamonds
with bright orange pupils.

Norbert Krapf

SYCAMORE ON MAIN STREET

It stands like a resolute
deserter of its own kind
high above frame houses
halfway up the hill.

Slowly, its brown mottled
bark has flaked away
leaving an ivory shaft
which glints in the sun.

Below the earth's surface,
its swollen roots crawl
homeward down the hillside,
wriggle beneath pipes
and pavement, plunge
into the depths, and suck
at the waters of the ancient
swamp beneath the park.

Norbert Krapf

COME INTO ANIMAL PRESENCE

Come into animal presence
No man is so guileless as
the serpent. The lonely white
rabbit on the roof is a star
twitching its ears at the rain.
The llama intricately
folding its hind legs to be seated
not disdains but mildly
disregards human approval.
What joy when the insouciant
armadillo glances at us and doesn't
quicken his trotting
across the track into the palm brush.

What is this joy? That no animal
falters, but knows what it must do?
That the snake has no blemish,
that the rabbit inspects his strange surroundings
in white star-silence? The llama
rests in dignity, the armadillo
has some intention to pursue in the palm-forest.
Those who were sacred have remained so,
holiness does not dissolve, it is a presence
of bronze, only the sight that saw it
faltered and turned from it.
An old joy returns in holy presence.

Denise Levertov

BY A GATOR CREEK CANAL
DURING THE DRY SEASON

A thin line of black-blue edged dark water
sluggish in a dry season canal.
The clouds that want to walk on water
cannot find footroom
and return to the sky
to lean on hidden stones.
You pause on the bank
pick up the loose sand
and its bits of stiff leaves
and let its warmth and roughness
slide through the fingers.
The fingers disappear in the flow
and the flow disappears
in the immobility of the fingers.
The barks of thoughts chased away
by the bones of light
that the sun put in the grasses.
A brown dragonfly hovers
over a three-petaled
mica-eyed blue flower.
The slant of his wings sends out
a flash of bronze gold,
and the flash turns you into rain.
All the sandgrains stand up.

Duane Locke

AN EVENING SPENT ON A GEORGIA FARM

The comets restless, their hay uneaten,
their hoofs kick against the boards of their stalls
The barn is too small for all this light.

The sky is almost dark.
All left on the horizon are the slim yellow hairs
dropped from the mane of the horses who
galloped into infinity.

Duane Locke

A NIGHT IN LATE DECEMBER

This starfish dry and brittle. It is strange
to meet it
here
on painted wood,
under desk light,
not under the five hundred moons
that its wet, pulsating body creates.
It leaves no tracks here.
It has a human face
under its stomach
and is trying to ply inside.
It pauses
as if asking for another food.

Her hands against the closed windows
the gulf presses her wild colored infinite fingers.

I go outside and crawl
under the rain heavy thick dark pine branches
and meet
directly before me
a chipmunk who was a flower,
a large
brown fungus
jumped up
from the oak roots.

The fungus arched its soft back
and rubbed against my night.

Duane Locke

RUNNING HORSE

A black horse
whose forward motion

sweeps tail and mane like charcoal
across the winter

pasture
is running parallel

to the highway
its hooves strike fire beneath

its belly
For a quarter mile

our heartbeats coax
Come ON!

Come ON!
but the horse swerves

through a gate, toward a hushed
Sunday barn

Assured it is still
Horse

it rears, and the nostrils close
It sought exercise

not freedom
Tomorrow

the horse's master
will repair the broken rails, grumbling

We drive on
Our hearts strike fire beneath

our bellies
over the frozen land

Steven Osterlund

A BUTTERFLY

Adhered by its own juice to a
Styrofoam

cup
the butterfly

mistook a windshield for more
air

I have brought it
inside—

beautiful
rust tan and star-speckled; its weight is

zero
the wings crumpled

A Japanese artist would
bow

I sit, quiet
for when I breathe

the butterfly
flutters across the table; behind

my eyes
it completes a cycle

beautifully
Until the wings disintegrate

I will keep it
On the curb

the cup is eternal, and feels
nothing

Steven Osterlund

TIGER

He lay
under slices
of white bread like a
rotten awning; all afternoon
his tongue sizzled
his shabby mouth twitched
his lean tail absently picked up
a wad of blue candy floss—

the cage
rife with absurd
ornaments: whirligigs
straws, Polaroid negatives

O tiger
I whispered
*the great rivers
of India!* Unable
to answer—a faded bunch
of suspenders; pigeon plaything

When I force him
out of my indignant mind
he often stalks through my dreams
much younger
Wicked as native grief
Gorged on sex and a startled
villager

Steven Osterlund

50.

RISING EARLY IN WINTER

Wild lake snow has heaved down
all night without sound.
Here, it is dawn.

A farmer walks around
in the thin yellow light
near the barn. Half asleep,
the sweet vegetable smell
of cows fills everything
with longing, the black trees,
his slow sons.

I suddenly know
that I love this winter,
it is a dark friend,
cold has the strongest arms.

Anthony Piccione

CAMPING ALONE

I lift
a small stone.
Something hurries
toward home. One
thin note is lost,
child or fox.

Moss root pressed
to mouth, I smell
women by a fire.
One kneels, pushes
wood into the center.
We see past each other,
slow memory of sun's thought
steaming through rock:
now, first, breathe,
wake. Take nothing.
Ice will come. Breathe,
think, think of leaving.

We are drifting toward home.
Stones disappear,
planets and sun fall back
through the ice. This is one dream.
Already we sense others.

Anthony Piccione

LATE AUTUMN

Kneeling mindless in a field
you suddenly feel
through bone
the great underground darkness.
Roots drop straight down
like any man,
falling from sleep.

Anthony Piccione

POEM TOUCHING THE FEET

Walking alone, sometimes,
in late afternoon
I'll feel that faint ripple
through the earth
cast up from behind
to the backs of my heels.

It is a time of great joy,
my grandfather swimming
strongly below my life.
He looks straight ahead,
smiling. We both know
the way: it holds the
seed his father sent,
from the center,
where the mother waits.

Anthony Piccione

HUMAN, AVIAN
VEGETABLE BLOOD

Today, three days before Christmas,
I had planned to cut some berries
From the toyon bush in the yard.
For three years it has not done well.
This is the first year it produced
A decent crop. But this morning
A flock of thirty migrating
Robins appeared, and before noon
Every berry had been eaten.
This year we will buy our foliage
As usual, and the symbols
Of incarnate flesh we tended
All year will be flying, mingled
With pale hot bird blood, high over
The barren Mexican mountains.

Kenneth Rexroth

ANOTHER SPRING

The seasons revolve and the years change
With no assistance or supervision.
The moon, without taking thought,
Moves in its cycle, full, crescent, and full.

The white moon enters the heart of the river;
The air is drugged with azalea blossoms;
Deep in the night a pine cone falls;
Our campfire dies out in the empty mountains.

The sharp stars flicker in the tremulous branches;
The lake is black, bottomless in the crystalline night;
High in the sky the Northern Crown
Is cut in half by the dim summit of a snow peak.

O heart, heart, so singularly
Intransigent and corruptible,
Here we lie entranced by the starlit water,
And moments that should each last forever

Slide unconsciously by us like water.

Kenneth Rexroth

HUNTING SEASON

The bed is the wrong bed.
The house is all wrong.

One by one,
The birds lift their nests
Away from the eaves

Flying sadly away.
Slowly, the animals
Walk backwards into the woods

And the pines walk back
Into the clouds.
There is a thick, thick fog.

The compass rusts.

It is the first day
Of open season.
They will be hunted down

And they touch each other's faces
For the last time
Like braille.

Susan Fromberg Schaeffer

ORDER

The black dot is missing
From the heights of the sky.

The heart of the mouse
Misses the heart of the hawk.

One eye on the carcass
One eye on the sky
It eats, overwhelmed

In white light.

The black sun is gone.

Say, what is this carcass?
Only the dead are immortal
And they are only temporary.

They stand before the white sun,
The red sun, clipped
To the rim of a hill

The keyholes, the black silhouettes.

Only the past is immortal
As long as you are.

Why pity the wolves
Asleep in their ice
Absolution on their fangs
Covered with blood?

When the world is hard,
And wide,
We have each other.

Oceans separate us
On our cracked egg.
The continents,
The cracked skull plates,
They never knit.

We die for the animals' innocence
We die feathered in deaths
Furred in deaths
Each finger a death-statue
The likeness perfect

As we age, they keep growing
Then we count with our toes

Oh God who sends the lemmings
To the cliff in packs
See the humans in their pink skins
Stumbling to the rim

Wild and alone,
One at a time,
One at a time.

Susan Fromberg Schaeffer

BURIAL GROUND

Elephant-skinned trees, a tumble
Of cold stones, a litter of leaves
And beyond these, the cemetery's
Neat grey rows.
Against a pale grey sky
A stone-cold angel lifts her granite hands,
Her full skirts
Unruffled by the wintry breeze, and at her feet
A small squirrel buries his sweet fruit.
He does not mark the place with stone
Or twig, nor do his beady eyes read
The inscription on the stone.
He knows what he knows.
The nut will be dug up.
The roots of the tree go deep,
They remember the sun and the rain.
We have no roots. We do not remember long.
We bury our dead
And carve their names in stone.

Susan Fromberg Schaeffer

RECUPERATION

My room has become my hospital room.
My only visitors are the cats.

They come in one at a time.
None of them stay too long.

All day, my nurse, my green tree
Flutters its balinesque hands
In the motions of a sophisticated dance.

It stands up straight.
Underneath, are the brown bones of twigs.
It shows me what has to be done.

Susan Fromberg Shaeffer

POEM WATCHING IN WINTER

set yr clock at 3 AM
to drive to western
Massachusetts

disregard the weather
forecast but wear
hiking boots, parka

dont forget yr field
guide, binoculars,
chocolate bars

head yr car to Grey-
lock Mountain & park
right in the road

no one else will face
the storm

then push yr way into
the forest
& dig a nest of snow

wait . . .

sooner or later
the Great Horned Owl
will come

Joanne Seltzer

62.

LONG HAIR

Hunting season:

Once every year, the Deer catch human beings. They do various things which irresistably draw men near them; each one selects a certain man. The Deer shoots the man, who is then compelled to skin it and carry its meat home and eat it. Then the Deer is inside the man. He waits and hides in there, but the man doesn't know it. When enough Deer have occupied enough men, they will strike all at once. The men who don't have Deer in them will also be taken by surprise, and everything will change some. This is called "takeover from inside."

Gary Snyder

THE DEAD BY THE SIDE OF THE ROAD

How did a great Red-tailed Hawk
　　come to lie—all stiff and dry—
　　　　on the shoulder of
　　　　　　Interstate 5?

Her wings for dance fans

Zac skinned a skunk with a crushed head
　　washed the pelt in gas; it hangs,
　　　　tanned, in his tent

Fawn stew on Hallowe'en
　　hit by a truck on highway forty-nine
　　　　offer cornmeal by the mouth;
　　　　　　skin it out.

Log trucks run on fossil fuel

I never saw a Ringtail til I found one in the road;
　　case-skinned it with the toenails
　　　　footpads, nose, and whiskers on;
　　　　　　it soaks in salt and water
　　　　　　sulphuric acid pickle;

she will be a pouch for magic tools.

The Doe was apparently shot
　　lengthwise and through the side—
　　　　shoulder and out the flank
　　　　　　belly full of blood

Can save the other shoulder maybe,
   if she didn't lie too long—
Pray to their spirits. Ask them to bless us:
   our ancient sisters' trails
      the roads were laid across and kill them:
         night-shining eyes

The dead by the side of the road.

Gary Snyder

SWANS

As a stranger wails his first cry
I walk past a lake of swans;
they are my sisters, gentle
ones who cannot speak,
the question marks of beauty:
like clouds following the wind
they nod to their subjects
and glide toward the banks,
opening the gates of the womb
for their white children.

David Spicer

ROOK

Under the moon a round cracker
a soft statue with feathers
peers from treeless hills
head perched up like a hooked fish
silently blessing stars with a frozen beak
darker than the raven night itself
and a shadow of the universe
immortal as the ghost of a god
who thinks of alternatives
at sunrise flying to a deserted beach
to rest beside a child's castle
with silent waves beating against its doors
a black bird content once again
the pet of holy hags listening
to the wind cry in pain for him
the last animal to choke and die
and the day remaining the day
as the sun begins to flow forever

David Spicer

THE ANTLER

It can be anything your eyes carve
a pipe to smoke on a sleepy day
a ventricle of the earth's snowy heart

Its folklore changes homes with every eclipse
slipping out the door with a hitchhiker
or falling from a pickup onto your hood

In the forest of snow near a tree
it might be the claw of a hawk
or the imprint of a new letter
in an alphabet of white woods

You know it belongs at the gravesight
for when the animal feels part of him missing
he will return for the bones of his soul
his pass key to high country

On a dark mountain you will face him
with music from the cold moon
tossing it toward him to vanish
odor of marrow in you forever
hooves over hills and dust in your smile
even the wind stepping aside

David Spicer

THE DAY I BECAME A VEGETARIAN

I woke from a dream that all my friends were scallions
I heard bravos from the lumps of beef I had left behind
From the ground round porterhouse and tartar
As they cleaved like peas and sent out shoots

The sprouts I had eaten
Rejoiced within the striations of my iris
Arched in delight tickling tight curls of chromosomes

I read leaves in a wadded lettuce heart
   for news of the world
I dug up sweet tuberous poems
I discovered myself counting the chambers in a tomato
I made ink from spores I signed my checks with it

The day I became a vegetarian
I found letters from all the fish in the seas

Frederick E. Steinway

FARMER

Seasons waiting the miracle,
dawn after dawn framing
the landscape in his eyes:

bound tight as wheat, packed
hard as dirt. Made shrewd
by soil and weather, through

the channel of his bones
shift ways of animals,
their matings twist his dreams.

While night-fields quicken,
shadows slanting right, then left
across the moonlit furrows,

he shelters in the farmhouse
merged with trees, a skin of wood,
as much the earth's as his.

Lucien Stryk

CORMORANT

Men speak lightly of frustration,
As if they'd invented it.

As if like the cormorant
of Gifu, thick leg roped, a ring

Cutting into the neck, they dived
All night to the fish-swelled water

And flapped up with the catch lodged
In the throat, only to have

The fisher yank it out and toss
It gasping on a breathless heap.

Then to dive again, hunger
Churning in the craw, air just

Slipping by the throat-ring
To spray against the lungs.

And once more to be jerked back in
And have the fisher grab the spoil.

Men speak lightly of frustration,
and dim in the lantern light

The cormorant makes out the flash
Of fins and, just beyond,

The steamered boats of tourists
Rocking under *sake* fumes.

Lucien Stryk

BLACK LEAVES

Once, in a field,
in the black shade of an oak,
an open coffin filling with leaves.

You want to sleep there forever,
surrounded by crickets
coaxing their sad, imaginary violins.

Say it's Sunday, the sky gone
white with staring. All morning
you've imagined nothing but heat,

the slow pressure of perspiration
on your wrist. You might start counting
sparrows confused in the valley,

but the coffin interrupts your romance
like a mother. So you circle
twice, making sure

there's been no mistake. Perhaps
this coffin belongs to your neighbor.
Perhaps it arrived by mail

years ago, was lost in revival,
abandoned in the cellar like preserves.
But the heat is blossoming, there's

too much to think, the red silk
rustles like something cool & the leaves,
the black leaves,

are falling one by one
until you can no longer resist, so
you slip in & sleep like nothing at all.

Michael Waters

IF I DIE

If I die, I would like to come back.
Those trees planted in the garden
might be grown, blooming.
Nothing dead

would inhabit their bright plot.
I would come back to taste
the apples hanging from a black
branch, each one

small, round, almost perfect,
a bag of blood,
a bullet-hole in the air,
the wound already closing.

If I could, I would come back
to the house settling on the marsh,
the slow curve of the hill
rising, now, like heaven.

I would place my grey lips
on the cold pane,
on the silhouette of a woman
who stops, alert, listening...

and I would lie down, again,
in this familiar portion of earth,
a guest among the trees,
and dream each night of coming back...

Michael Waters

74.

REMEMBERING THE OAK

I have taught my son to hammer nails,
barely, into the tree. He believes
squirrels need help
climbing.

If the owl in that tree remembers
field-mice offering themselves
on tables of fresh snow,
if the oak

memorizes each brown leaf like a son,
perhaps my son will remember
this nailing business
years from now.

He'll be hammering his own stubborn
nails into boards, sweating
like Christ in the sun,
thumbs blackening,

when the leaves above him will whisper
with the rustling of an owl.
He'll remember the oak,
still growing

from the soil in southern Ohio,
the nails climbing the trunk
like furious locusts,
the father

who held his fist like the first
spring leaf, who remains
rooted like memory
in the earth.

Michael Waters

WHEN THERE WERE TREES

I can remember when there were trees,
great tribes of spruces who deckled themselves in light,
beeches buckled in pewter, meeting like Quakers,
the golden birch, all cutwork satin,
courtesan of the mountains; the paper birch
trying all summer to take off its clothes
like the swaddlings of the newborn.

The hands of a sassafras blessed me.
I saw maples fanning the fire in their stars,
heard the coins of the aspens rattling like teeth,
saw cherry trees spraying fountains of light,
smelled the wine my heel pressed from ripe apples,
saw a thousand planets bobbing like bells
on the sleeve of the sycamore, chestnut, and lime.

The ancients knew that a tree is worthy of worship.
A few wise men from their tribes broke through the sky,
climbing past worlds to come and the rising moon
on the patient body of the tree of life,
and brought back the souls of the newly slain,
no bigger than apples, and dressed the tree
as one of themselves and danced.

Even the conquerors of this country
lifted their eyes and found the trees
more comely than gold: *Bright green trees,*
and whole land so green it is pleasure to look on it
and the greatest wonder to see the diversity.
During that time, I walked among trees,
the most beautiful things I had ever seen. *

Watching the shadows of trees, I made peace with mine.
Their forked darkness gave motion to morning light.
Every night the world fell to the shadows,
and every morning came home, the dogwood floating
its petals like moons on a river of air,
the oak kneeling in wood sorrel and fern,
the willow washing its hair in the stream.

And I saw how the logs from the mill floated
downstream, saw otters and turtles that rode them,
and though I heard the saws whine in the woods
I never thought men were stronger than trees.
I never thought those tribes would join their brothers,
the buffalo and the whale, the leopard, the seal, the
    wolf,
and the men of this country who knew how to sing
    them.

Nothing I ever saw washed off the sins of the world
so well as the first snow dropping on trees.
We shoveled the pond clear and skated under their
    branches,
our voices muffled in their huge silence.
The trees were always listening to something else.
They didn't hear the beetle with the hollow tooth
grubbing for riches, gnawing for empires, for gold.

Already the trees are a myth,
half gods, half giants in whom nobody believes.
But I am the oldest woman on earth,
and I can remember when there were trees.

Nancy Willard

*Adpated from the journals of Christopher Columbus, as
rendered in William Carlos Williams' *In The American Grain*.

MOSS

A green sky underfoot:
the skin of moss
holds the footprints of
star-footed birds.

With moss-fingers, with
filigree they line
their nests in the
forks of the trees.

All around the apples
are falling, the leaves
snap, the sun moves
away from the earth.

Only the moss stays,
decently covers the
roots of things, itself
rooted in silence:

rocks coming alive
_underfoot, rain no
man heard fall. Moss,
stand up for us,

the small birds and
the great sun. You know
our trees and apples,
our parrots and women's eyes.

Keep us in your green
body, laid low
and still blossoming
under the snow.

Nancy Willard

IRIS

The iris shoot unsheathes
itself crumpled and wet
as the folds of a stomach,

then straightens, summoned
into the elegant blades,
sealed, calked, one on

the other, a print of
leaves, brushed on the
air. This is the tongue

of marriage: we grow,
we cleave without asking.
With our skin

we know.

Nancy Willard

MILKWEED

While I stood here, in the open, lost in myself,
I must have looked a long time
Down the corn rows, beyond grass,
The small house,
White walls, animals, lumbering toward the barn.
I look down now. It is all changed.
Whatever it was I lost, whatever I wept for
Was a wild, gentle thing, the small dark eyes
Loving me in secret.
It is here. At a touch of my hand,
The air fills with delicate creatures
From the other world.

James Wright

A BLESSING

Just off the highway to Rochester, Minnesota,
Twilight bounds softly forth on the grass.
And the eyes of those two Indian ponies
Darken with kindness.
They have come gladly out of the willows
To welcome my friend and me.
We step over the barbed wire into the pasture
Where they have been grazing all day, alone.
They ripple tensely, they can hardly contain their
    happiness
That we have come.
They bow shyly as wet swans. They love each other.
There is no loneliness like theirs.
At home once more,
They begin munching the young tufts of spring in the
    darkness.
I would like to hold the slenderer one in my arms,
For she has walked over to me
And nuzzled my left hand.
She is black and white,
Her mane falls wild on her forehead,
And the light breeze moves me to caress her long ear
That is delicate as the skin over a girl's wrist.
Suddenly I realize
That if I stepped out of my body I would break
Into blossom.

James Wright

81.

FEAR IS WHAT QUICKENS ME

I.

Many animals that our fathers killed in America
Had quick eyes.
They stared about wildly,
When the moon went dark.
The new moon falls into the freight yards
Of cities in the south,
But the loss of the moon to the dark hands of Chicago
Does not matter to the deer
In this northern field.

II.

What is that tall woman doing
There, in the trees?
I can hear rabbits and mourning doves whispering
    together
In the dark grass, there
Under the trees.

III.

I look about wildly.

James Wright

CONTRIBUTORS

SUSAN ASTOR'S poetry has appeared in *The Chowder Review*, *The Paris Review*, *Carolina Quarterly*, and in *Shaping: New Poems in Traditionally Prossodies*, (Dryad Press, 1978). Poems of hers will appear shortly in *Shenandoah*, *Poetry Now*, *New Collage Magazine* and *The Carleton Miscellany*.

ROBERT BLY, born in 1926, has received numerous honors for his poetry and translations. He is the founder of The Seventies Press and the creator of the annual "Conference on The Great Mother and The New Father." His most recent translation is *The Voices* by Rainer Maria Rilke (Ally Press, 1977) and forthcoming is a new collection from the work of Antonio Machado (Ally Press).

JOE BRUCHAC lives with his wife Carol and their two sons in the Adirondack foothills, in Greenfield Center, New York. There they work garden earth which was planted by his grandfather for five decades before them. His most recent books include a novel, *The Dreams of Jessie Brown* (Cold Mountain Press); a collection of Iroquois folktales, *Stone Giants and Flying Heads* (Crossing Press); and two chapbooks, *M'Undu Wi Go* (Blue Cloud Quarterly) and *There Are No Trees In The Prison* (Blackberry Press); all published in 1978.

PHILIP DACEY, born in 1939, was educated at St. Louis University, Stanford, and the University of Iowa. His work has appeared in numerous periodicals and anthologies, including *Esquire*, *American Review*, *Poetry* (Chicago), *Paris Review*, *The Nation* and *The American Poetry Anthology*. The recipient of many awards and fellowships, he teaches creative writing at Southwest State University in Minnesota and lives in Cottonwood with his wife and three children. He has published one book of poems, *How I Escaped From The Labyrinth And Other Poems* (Carnegie-Mellon University Press, 1977).

W.D. EHRHART is co-editor of *Demilitarized Zones: Veterans After Vietnam*, and author of three Samisdat chapbooks: *A Generation of Peace, Rootless,* and *Empire.* He teaches at Sandy Spring Friends School in Maryland.

CHARLES FISHMAN is co-founder of the Long Island Poetry Collective, and founding editor of *Xanadu Magazine* and Pleasure Dome Press. His books include: *Aurora* (Tree Books, 1974), *Mortal Companions* (Pleasure Dome Press, 1977) and *Warm-Blooded Animals* (Juniper Press, 1977). Recent work has appeared in *The Hollins Critic, The Greenfield Review, Shir Hadash* and others.

FRANK GRAZIANO, 23, has published four chapbooks of poetry: *Walhalla* (S.C. Arts Commission); *Desemboque* (Floating Island); *Follain* (The Bieler Press); shared with prose of Jean Follain; and *Duncan, The Potato Eaters & Thanksgiving in the Shadow of Goat-Tit Mountain* (The duBois Zone Press). He is the founder of Grilled Flowers Press and is a graduate student at the University of Iowa.

MARJORIE HAWKSWORTH teaches creative writing in Santa Barbara. Poems of hers have appeared recently in *Poetry Northwest, Southern Poetry Review, Sou'wester, Poet and Critic, Chelsea* and *Gravida.*

WILLIAM HEYEN'S most recent book is *The Swastika Poems* (Vanguard Press, 1978). Recent chapbooks include *The Ash* (Banjo Press); *Lord Dragonfly* (Rock Press); and *From This Book of Praise* (Street Press). Vanguard will publish *Long Island Light: Poems and a Memoir* in 1979.

A native Kansan, WILLIAM KLOEFKORN has published two books of poetry, *Alvin Turner As Farmer* (Windflower Press, 1974) and *Uncertain The Final Run To Winter* (Windflower Press, 1974). He is assistant professor of English at Nebraska Wesleyan University, is married and has four children.

TED KOOSER was born in 1939 in Ames, Iowa and was educated at Iowa State University and the University of Nebraska. He works as an underwriter in Lincoln, Nebraska, where he edits Windflower Press. He has two book length collections in print, *A local habitation & a name* (Solo Press, 1974), and *Not Coming To Be Barked At* (Pentagram Press, 1976).

NORBERT KRAPF was born in Jasper, Indiana in 1943 and lives in Roslyn, New York. A chapbook of poems, *The Playfair Book of Hours* appeared in 1976 (Ally Press), and *Finding The Grain*, a collection of pioneer journals, Franconian folktales and poems was published in 1977 by the Dubois County Historical Society and Herald Printing, Inc. He teaches at the C.W. Post Center of Long Island University.

DENISE LEVERTOV was born in England in 1923 and was privately educated at home. She has been Poetry Editor for *The Nation*, a teacher, and a recipient of a grant from the National Institute of Arts and Letters. Her books of poetry include *The Jacob's Ladder*, *The Sorrow Dance*, and *Relearning the Alphabet*, all published by New Directions.

DUANE LOCKE was born on a farm near Plains, Georgia and was educated at the University of Florida. He teaches English at the University of Tampa and has appeared in over 400 magazines including *The Nation*, *Ann Arbor Review*, and *Kansas Quarterly*. He is the founder of the "Immanentist" school of poetry and has had ten small press books of poems published.

STEVEN OSTERLUND, born in Ohio, moved to Canada in 1967 to avoid the draft. He returned to Ohio in 1978 and is writing a long prose work on his experiences as an exile. Books in print include *Twenty Love Poems* (Windflower Press); *Pendulum* (Open Chord Press); *Black Ice* (Open Chord Press); and forthcoming is *The French Detective*, prose poems and drawings (Open Chord Press).

ANTHONY PICCIONE lives in Kendall, New York and teaches at the State University of New York-Brockport. He has published one book of poems, *Anchor Dragging* (Boa Editions, 1977).

KENNETH REXROTH was born in 1905 in South Bend, Indiana and grew up in Chicago. Having quit school at 16 he worked various jobs, including logging and journalism. He is the author of several books of translations and books of his own verse, including *The Collected Shorter Poems* and *The Collected Longer Poems*. He has lived most of his life in San Francisco and now lives in Santa Barbara.

SUSAN FROMBERG SCHAEFFER was born in Brooklyn in 1941, was educated at the University of Chicago and is a full professor of English at Brooklyn College. She has published two novels and several collections of poetry, including *Granite Lady* (Macmillan, 1974); *Alphabet for the Lost Years* (Gallimaufry, 1976); and a chapbook, *The Red White and Blue Poem* (Ally Press, 1977). She is married and has one son.

JOANNE SELTZER was born in the old Jewish section of Detroit, spent most of the nineteen-fifties in western Massachusetts, and has lived since in Schenectady, New York. She began to write in 1973 and has published poetry in a wide variety of magazines, including *The Cimarron Review, Poetry Now, The Minnesota Review, The Village Voice* and others. She is the winner of the fifth "All Nations Poetry Contest," sponsored by Triton College.

GARY SNYDER was born in 1930 in San Francisco and was educated at Reed, Berkeley, Indiana and a Japanese Zen monastery. He has worked as a logger, forest ranger and seaman. Included in his many books is *Turtle Island* (New Directions, 1974) which won the Pulitzer Prize for Poetry in 1975.

DAVID SPICER is editor of *racoon*, a magazine of poetry, reviews and translations published in Memphis, Tennessee by St. Luke's Press. He has had poems appear in *Poetry Now, Aura, Road Apple Review, Moondance* and other magazines. He has published one chapbook, *The Beast's Remembered* (Bozart Press, 1977).

FREDRICK STEINWAY lives in New York City where he has a job with Law Publishing. His work has recently appeared in *Psychological Perspectives, The Nantucket Review* and *Telephone*.

LUCIEN STRYK grew up in Chicago and is the editor of *Heartland* and *Heartland II: Poets of the Midwest*. He has published six books of poetry including *Awakening* (1973), winner of the 1974 Society of Midland Authors Poetry Award, and *Selected Poems* (The Swallow Press, 1976). He has given poetry readings throughout the United States and England, has been a visiting lecturer in Japan and Iran, and presently teaches at Northern Illinois University.

MICHAEL WATERS teaches at Salisbury State College in Maryland. Ithica House published *Fish Light* in 1975 and a new book, *Not Just Any Death*, is due soon from BOA Editions. His poems have appeared in *Poetry, American Poetry Review, Georgia Review, Iowa Review, Rolling Stone* and other periodicals.

NANCY WILLARD teaches in the English Department at Vassar College. She has published several volumes of poetry, criticism and fiction, including her most recent book, *The Highest Hit*, published by Harcourt Brace Jovanovich.

JAMES WRIGHT was born in Martin's Ferry, Ohio, in 1927, and was educated at Kenyon College and the University of Washington-Seattle. An English teacher at Hunter College in New York City, Wright's poetry first achieved national recognition in 1957 when he won the Yale Series of Younger Poets Award. Since then his work has collected many other honors, including the Pulitzer Prize in 1972 for his *Collected Poems*.

The editor, PAUL FEROE, was born in Duluth, Minnesota, 1951, and graduated from St. Olaf College. For the past five years he has lived in Denver where he worked as a journalist, bank clerk and vegetarian activist. He now lives in St. Paul and is employed as a printer.